INFLUENCE

Portable Power for the '90s

Elaina Zuker

A FIFTY-MINUTE™ SERIES BOOK

CRISP PUBLICATIONS, INC.
Menlo Park, California

D1279112

INFLUENCE

Portable Power for the '90s

Elaina Zuker

CREDITS:
Layout and Composition: **Interface Studio**
Cover Design: **Carol Harris**
Artwork: **Ralph Mapson**

Copyright © 1994 Elaina Zuker
Printed in the United States of America.

English language Crisp books are distributed worldwide. Our major international distributors include:

CANADA: Reid Publishing, Ltd., Box 69559—109 Thomas St., Oakville, Ontario, Canada L6J 7R4. TEL: (416) 842-4428, FAX: (416) 842-9327

AUSTRALIA: Career Builders, P. O. Box 1051, Springwood, Brisbane, Queensland, Australia 4127. TEL: 841-1061, FAX: 841-1580

NEW ZEALAND: Career Builders, P. O. Box 571, Manurewa, Auckland, New Zealand. TEL: 266-5276, FAX: 266-4152

JAPAN: Phoenix Associates Co., Mizuho Bldg. 2-12-2, Kami Osaki, Shinagawa-Ku, Tokyo 141, Japan. TEL: 3-443-7231, FAX: 3-443-7640

Selected Crisp titles are also available in other languages. Contact International Rights Manager Suzanne Kelly at (415) 323-6100 for more information.

Library of Congress Catalog Card Number 93-73458
Zuker, Elaina
Influence
ISBN 1-56052-275-5

This book is printed on recyclable paper with soy ink.

ABOUT THIS BOOK

Influence: Portable Power for the '90s is not like most books. It has a unique self-paced format that encourages a reader to become personally involved. Designed to be "read with a pencil," there are exercises, activities, assessments and cases that invite participation.

This book is designed to help you understand and identify your individual style of influence and how you and others process information. This information will enhance your communication and listening skills to become a more powerful influence and get people to trust you and support your ideas.

Influence: Portable Power for the '90s can be used effectively in a number of ways. Here are some possibilities:

- **Individual Study.** Because the book is self-instructional, all that is needed is a quiet place, some time and a pencil. Completing the activities and exercises will provide valuable feedback, as well as practical ideas for improving your business and interpersonal successes.

- **Workshops and Seminars.** This book is ideal for use during, or as pre-assigned reading prior to, a workshop or seminar. With the basics in hand, the quality of participation will improve. More time can be spent practicing concept extensions and applications during the program.

- **College Programs.** Thanks to the format, brevity and low cost, this book is ideal for short courses and extension programs.

There are other possibilities that depend on the objectives of the user. One thing is certain: even after it has been read, this book will serve as excellent reference material that can be easily reviewed.

ABOUT THE AUTHOR

A seasoned business woman, educator, writer, and consultant, Ms. Zuker has held executive positions in publishing, higher education, manufacturing, and communications.

Her newest book, *The Seven Secrets of Influence* (McGraw-Hill), the recent Main Selection for the Business Week Book Club, is slated to be translated into seven languages. She is also the author of *Mastering Assertiveness Skills* and *The Assertive Manager* (AMACOM). She has been featured on numerous radio and television talk shows and in many newspaper articles. She has created custom publications for *TIME, Money, Home Mechanix, Inc., Working Woman,* and many other magazines.

She has served on the faculties of Montclair State College (Division of Business), Mercy College, Pace University, and Marymount College.

She is director of the National Association for Female Executives' Membership Drive. She has been a keynote speaker at Organization Development Network, American Society for Training and Development, Direct Selling Association, International Association of Business Communicators, Hotel Sales and Marketing Association International, and Association of Association Executives.

She holds a B.S. in Psychology (Empire State College, NY) and an M.S. in Organizational Behavior/Management (NY Polytechnic Institute).

Elaina Zuker

CONTENTS

INTRODUCTION

The idea for this book came from a seminar I created and conducted with groups of managers and professionals in corporations all over America. It's based on real work with real people who need real hands-on skills to help them in their daily interactions, as they attempt to work together in the increasingly tough and competitive environments of most organizations today.

With a team of organizational psychologists, I did some research, interviewing people in different groups and departments. I discovered that most training programs were directed at managers or executives. The training that was offered to professionals and "individual contributors" was usually informational, intended to help them further develop their technical skills.

What they really needed to complete their proficiency in managing and completing projects was the missing skill—influence skill. As a result, I developed an influence skills program and then a *train the trainer* program, for a wider audience.

There are many benefits to learning about influence skills, including:

- Understanding how people process information and tuning in to the information processing strategies different people use so you can become a more powerful influencer

- Learning refined listening skills and finely tuned attentiveness

- Discovering other people's decision making strategies

- Enhancing your ability to facilitate other people's decisions

- Having a more flexible behavioral repertoire

PART

I

Influence—
Getting What You Want

INFLUENCE—
GETTING WHAT YOU WANT

Influence. Everyone wants it. But how do you get it? Like the weather, influence is usually noticed only by its outcome. When you've changed someone's mind or opinion, you notice the change. But the methods or strategies you used are usually instinctive. You often aren't sure of exactly what you did that worked.

Since we generally aren't aware of how we influence other people, it's easy to believe that this ability is a mysterious gift or talent. You either have it or you don't have it. Or you may believe that influence is a privilege exercised only by those who already wield power.

But anyone can have influence. Influence is a set of interpersonal skills that can be learned, practiced, and mastered.

What Influences You?

It's easy to see influence as a process if you think of a personal situation. Think of a time when you were influenced, when someone was able to change your opinion, attitude, or behavior. Maybe a teacher helped you meet a special challenge or a friend convinced you to buy one car rather than another.

- Try to recall what that person said or did to influence you.

- Which of your triggers or "hot buttons" were pushed?

- Were you painted a brighter vision of the future?

- Were there words or phrases that influenced you?

- Close your eyes and replay the scene in your mind and recall the verbal and nonverbal communication.

- Were you offered a reward?

- Was logic used?

Exercise: What Influences You?

To learn how to influence others, start by understanding how you yourself are influenced.

1. The person who influenced me was: _____

   _____

   _____

   _____

2. I was influenced to (do, think, change, believe): _____

   _____

   _____

   _____

3. The key reasons I was influenced were (for example, to maintain the status quo, to face reality, to take the practical course, to accept the person's future vision, financial reward, fear of loss, prospect of good relationship, etc.):

   _____

   _____

   _____

   _____

   _____

4. The words and phrases that influenced me were: _____

   _____

   _____

   _____

   _____

   _____

   _____

   _____

Influence Factors Checklist

Power may be something that has influenced you. You may have been influenced by the desire to fulfill a goal. The goal of this exercise is for you to begin to discover what influences you. All of what influences you may not be on the list. And what influences you one day may not appeal to you the next. Do the best you can with the clues provided to trigger your memory.

Below is a list of values or tendencies that many people say are the kinds of things that influence them. Completing this list will help you understand what influences you. You may also realize you are influenced by things not on this list.

I am influenced by:	Yes	No
Those I trust	——	——
Good rapport	——	——
Logic, data, or analysis	——	——
An appeal to my intuition	——	——
Authority or power in another person	——	——
The chance to use my own power and authority	——	——
Money	——	——
Anger	——	——
Rewards	——	——
Threats	——	——
Maintaining the status quo	——	——
A consensus among others	——	——
The chance to be happy	——	——
Thrill or risk-taking	——	——
A sense of security	——	——
The chance to achieve	——	——
Competence or efficiency	——	——
Adventure	——	——
Friendship	——	——
Creativity	——	——
Moral or ethical arguments	——	——
The chance to help others or help society	——	——
Recognition	——	——
Independence	——	——
Practical considerations	——	——
The chance to benefit others	——	——
Other (please specify) _____		

A NEW DEFINITION OF INFLUENCE

What Influence Isn't

What exactly do we mean by *influence*? What is this quality that can inspire brilliant performance and motivate people? There are a lot of misconceptions about what influence is and what it isn't. One is that *influence* and *power* are synonymous. Power is certainly a form of influence, but it's often the least effective. That's because when a person relies on power alone to get results, in the long run others are unlikely to cooperate willingly and mutually beneficial relationships are unlikely to form.

Let's examine some common myths and misconceptions about influence.

> *Misconception: The most visible or vocal person is the most influential.*

Reality: Often the person who talks the most or is the most visible is not necessarily the most powerful. When people are talking or displaying themselves, their attention is focused inward and they are more likely to miss cues and information about the situation and other people. These are the very cues that are most necessary to influence others.

> *Misconception: Influence is the same as communication.*

Reality: Not everything you say and do is geared toward influencing someone. Sometimes we are simply getting along with people. Influence skills are a subset of communication skills used specifically to persuade someone else.

> *Misconception: Real managers don't need influence.*

Reality: Like real men don't eat quiche? That used to be true, but it isn't anymore, as we'll see. These days, *all* managers need to influence their subordinates more effectively. The old style of "command management" simply doesn't work anymore.

> *Misconception: Influence is manipulation.*

Reality: Some people use the words *influence* and *manipulation* interchangeably. Unfortunately, because the word manipulation carries such a heavy negative connotation, many people avoid the use of the word influence. But influence is not the same as manipulation. Manipulation is dishonest, overly aggressive actions designed to cause someone to change his or her belief or behavior to benefit the manipulator. The key word is *dishonest*.

WHAT INFLUENCE MEANS TO YOU

So what is influence? What does *influence* mean to you?

Write your definition of *influence* here: _____

_____

_____

_____

Now write down what you'd be able to accomplish if you have more
influence. How would things be different? _____

_____

_____

_____

Influence is the Ability to Affect Others—Seen Only in its Effect—Without Exertion of Force or Formal Authority.

To understand this definition better, let's examine its parts.

"The Ability to Affect Others . . ."

This is the *positive* use of power, the potential or capacity of influence. This power
is like electricity—it's only effective when you turn it on and put it into action.

" . . . Seen Only in Its Effect . . ."

In other words, *results*, not only methods, count. If you and your actions created a
difference, incurred a change, or made an impact, then you had influence. What
you did to create that change may not have been noticeable.

" . . . Without Exertion of Force or Formal Authority"

Influence is a gentle skill, a much more refined approach to affecting others than
the use of authority or coercion.

Any bully or power-crazed boss can force you to do something that's against your
natural inclination. But the change that results from force will only be short-term,
and such behavior breeds distrust and hostility over the long run. It takes *skill* to
truly influence for positive, long-term results for both sides.

DOVETAILING— YOUR WIN-WIN STRATEGY

INFLUENCE

Influence is a positive process. You get the results you want while allowing others to get the results they want. It's a mutually beneficial relationship. Your needs and outcomes dovetail with those of the other person. This dovetailing enables you to keep your own personal integrity while respecting the other person's integrity. Although you can't set other people's goals for them, you can help them get what they want while you're getting what you want.

Dovetailing is the smart way to ensure your own success. And it's key to understanding positive influencing. Other people become your allies rather than your saboteurs. If people can benefit from their relationship with you, they'll be more likely to help you achieve your goals. This is the most important feature of influence skills—your ability to create a win-win situation.

MANIPULATION

Manipulation is talking or acting without regard for other people's goals. It is distinctly different from the interpersonal dovetailing of influence.

The power of your communication is the result you get. If your communication is not getting you the results you want, then you need to alter your communication until you *do* see the outcome you want.

Earlier, we talked about using your instincts to discern manipulation. This ability to perceive motives, to understand the hidden desires of others, regardless of what is being said or done on the surface, is a vital influence skill.

People who develop this skill gain a great deal of self-understanding. They know what their goals are and become aware of their own strategies for fulfilling these goals. These skilled influencers learn to combine self-understanding with another important element, namely, self-confidence. These skills are the prerequisites of becoming an adept influencer.

Getting Tuned In

One of the most important influence skills is the ability to understand the true motives and desires of others *regardless of what is being said or done on the surface.* This finding supports our notion of trusting your uneasy feeling in communications with others, since these feelings often signal manipulation attempts. But the most skilled influencers are able to understand and empathize with others, whether the underlying motives of the others are positive or negative. Skilled influencers are simply tuned in.

Skilled influencers also have a great deal of self-understanding. They know what their own goals are, they know what they are aiming for, and they are aware of their own strategies. Skilled influencers combine empathy and self-understanding with two other important elements: self-confidence and a desire for authority. The result is a person who is able to reconcile his or her motives with those of others in order to meet deadlines or to move toward a solution to problems that are either obvious and stated or subtle and unspoken.

There Are No Shortcuts

Then there are the people who try to shortcut the influencing process. These shortcuts fall into distinct patterns of behavior, so it's important to watch out for them. You'll recognize these shortcuts because they create undue pressure. It isn't necessary to induce pressure if influence skills are used effectively.

Remember: Influence should be felt only in its effect, not by exertion of force.

Exercise: Formulating Your Personal Influence Goals

Before beginning any new enterprise, it's always a good idea to establish specific goals. Place a checkmark by the goals that may be appropriate to you to:

- ☐ "Read" other people and situations better.
- ☐ Be flexible.
- ☐ Get cooperation from previously adversarial individuals or groups.
- ☐ Persuade others to support projects.
- ☐ Get more information from people when it's needed.
- ☐ Have more credibility with others.
- ☐ See ideas inside as well as outside my immediate department or group.
- ☐ Communicate better within my department and with my manager.
- ☐ Listen and respond better to others.
- ☐ Learn new ideas and apply these ideas in communication.
- ☐ Communicate more effectively with others outside my immediate group.
- ☐ Become more effective at meetings.
- ☐ Keep meetings moving productively.
- ☐ Learn to get more information from people in my organization.
- ☐ Become more aware of and open to the different styles of those I work with.
- ☐ Learn how to create cooperation.
- ☐ Identify and expand my base of supporters.
- ☐ Get my projects supported by upper management.
- ☐ Become aware of more options, so I don't get "stuck."

What are your other goals? _____

_____

_____

_____

_____

CREATING A PERSONAL INFLUENCE ACTION PLAN

Do one or two people keep recurring on your checklist? Is there a particular goal you want to achieve?

An influence action plan will help you focus more specifically on your goals. You will be able to pinpoint a short-term, specific influence goal for that one person or situation that currently represents a challenge for you. Later, you may want to return to this plan to change, refine, or update it.

A FIVE-STEP PLAN

STEP 1   **TARGET the person or people to influence.**

Is it your boss? A peer? A subordinate? Or is it someone who has the power to stop your promotion or eliminate your pet project from the schedule?

STEP 2   **IDENTIFY the situation to be changed.**

Is it an action? Maybe it's inaction. Maybe you want this person to be more open with you. Or perhaps you would like to clear up a misunderstanding.

STEP 3   **ENVISION a positive outcome.**

Will you simply fulfill your immediate goal? Or will there be some long-term effect—either positive or negative?

STEP 4   **CREATE benchmarks to measure success.**

What measurable, observable evidence will you need to ensure that your goal has been fulfilled? Is the person more friendly now? More open to your suggestions? Measuring results is critical to gauging success. You'd be surprised at how many people overlook this very important aspect of influencing.

STEP 5   **SET deadlines.**

Determine when you can realistically expect to influence this person and fulfill your goal. It can be a year or six months from now—or even next week. But set a real date and stick to it.

This plan reminds you to achieve the goal you've set for yourself. You can also use this format as a model for setting future influence goals.

Exercise: Influence Action Plan

This exercise is designed to help you pinpoint a short-term, specific influence goal.

1. *Who* do I want to influence?

   _____

   _____

   _____

2. *What* behavior do I want to change in this person?

   _____

   _____

   _____

3. *What* will result if I manage to influence this change?

   _____

   _____

   _____

4. *How* will I know the result has been achieved?

   _____

   _____

   _____

5. *When* will I realistically influence this person and fulfill this goal?

   _____

   _____

   _____

PART

II

Influencing in an Age of Change

INFLUENCING IN AN AGE OF CHANGE

Every personal interaction is an influence interaction. We have already seen how powerful and important a skill influencing can be. Now let's look at some of the evidence that influencing is becoming a key skill in the current business environment.

Meeting the Challenge of an Age of Change

Whether you are a rookie in today's workplace or a seasoned veteran, you'll be playing by a different set of rules. Behind these changes are several new trends changing the way companies operate in the business world. There are six areas in which big changes are happening:

COMPETITION

TECHNOLOGY

INFORMATION

WORKER VALUES

INNOVATION

ORGANIZATION

COMPETITION:

The Race Heats Up

Companies in Transition

For corporations and companies of all sizes, the emphasis now is on *streamlining, downsizing, containing cost,* and *belt-tightening,* either to guard against takeovers
or to make the company more attractive to investors. The bottom line for employees: scarcer resources. You now face hotter and hotter competition with your colleagues for the basic resources, such as budgets, equipment, and support staff, that you need to do your job.

On a personal level, this trend means increased competition for project approvals, for choice assignments, for the attention of management, and for all the extras that you once may have taken for granted.

Competitiveness at Home and Abroad

Successfully competing within a company, however, won't mean anything unless your company itself is competitive. And today, influence that works is essential to maintaining competitiveness in national and world markets.

Influence skills are now a necessary part of the job, whether you're in marketing, public relations, sales, accounting, or purchasing. Knowing how to work well with people who control resources is to your advantage—and to your company's. Such skills are key to surviving in today's restrictive business atmosphere.

Cultural Diversity

There's another dimension to this picture. Your suppliers, buyers, investors, and partners may be from a different culture. You may now be doing business with foreign-owned companies, foreign subsidiaries of your own company, or with the overseas headquarters of your own company. Soon, you may be doing business with a unified European marketplace and with developing countries jockeying for position in the global economy.

All this means increased global competition. You'll be competing with and working for people who have different customs, cultural backgrounds, and communication habits. Finely tuned influence skills offer the only way to sure success in this new environment.

TECHNOLOGY:

The Danger Of Depersonalization

Our global economy is made possible by new communication technology, the second area of far-reaching change. These technologies, are completely changing how business is conducted. Today we are connected as never before.

Wanted: One-on-One Skills for the New Team Environment

The gap between the technically knowledgeable and the technologically naive continues to widen. As a result, people who have technical jobs work more often on multifunction teams or task forces. More jobs require interdepartmental teams, or teams made up of people who do not typically work together and who may not even work at the same job site.

But as John Naisbitt, author of the best-seller *Megatrends 2000*, points out, our high-tech capabilities have raced ahead of our ''high-touch'' needs. We are investing increasingly larger blocks of time and energy in learning how to use these new technologies most effectively. But as our communication becomes more technical, we are spending less time developing the interpersonal communication skills that enable us to produce the best product or provide the service that we can. You can't get agreement or support for what you want without communicating your desires clearly.

INFORMATION:

Getting What You Need

Try to imagine the marketplace 40 years ago. No copy machines, no overnight mail, and no modems to connect you with suppliers or clients. Managers had much less information to work with. Today's increase in technology has prompted a parallel increase in information. Information now comes to us in mind-boggling quantities and at split-second speeds. And as we rapidly move from an industrial economy based on manufacturing to a service economy, the flow of information only quickens.

Influencing Information Flow

Yet the problem is not the overflow of information but the distribution of this information throughout an organization. Getting information to the right person at the right time can mean the success or failure of major deals. And it can save enormous amounts of money that would otherwise be spent duplicating efforts. Getting all the information you need also presents new challenges.

It's like putting together a jigsaw puzzle. There are people who have some pieces of it. But in order to complete the puzzle—to get the whole picture—the rest of the pieces must be acquired from other people. The secret of success is being able to gain the cooperation of all the right people. And that's where influence comes in.

WORKER VALUES:

New Management Norms Required

In the not-too-distant past, individuals worked autonomously. We rarely knew what the next person up the ladder did in our company—much less what people did in other companies. Information on how we do our jobs has now become more accessible. We're not as secretive as we once were. There is less physical space and less job differentiation between us and the people below and above us.

As a result, employees are developing different job expectations. This represents a radical change in worker values.

Employees no longer tolerate bossy managers who act like dictators or commanding officers. Instead of simply following arbitrary orders, workers want to take part actively in decision making. This new expectation has created a need for a different type of manager.

The most successful managers today are more open and encourage participation and two-way communication. Managers who remain closed or secretive risk alienating people both above and below them in the coporate structure. Corporations now look for managers with the right people skills.

This management style is worn-out and unwelcome.

INNOVATION:

We're All Expected
to be More Creative

The new work force of more responsive and responsible workers and more open managers has increased the demand for internal innovation. More and more companies are demanding increased creativity from their workers in return for increased career control.

Companies are looking for innovative ideas concerning internal structure as well as external competition. Workers and managers are asked to become ''intrapreneurs''—innovators who work inside a corporate structure to create smaller business units which operate almost independently of the parent organization.

No longer is creativity the exclusive province of the marketing or advertising departments. In today's most successful companies, all areas—manufacturing, management information systems, accounting, human resources, and research and development—are hotbeds of innovation and creativity.

Successfully implementing these new ideas and creative solutions calls for highly developed communication and influence skills. The innovator needs the ability to sell an idea to the decision makers. We've all seen a great idea die a premature death or gather dust in a file drawer because its creator lacked influence skills.

MAKE INDIVIDUALITY WORK FOR YOU

ORGANIZATIONAL STRUCTURE:

Changing the Way
Things Work

The five trends discussed so far have contributed to a sixth change, namely, reorganization. Corporations are now undergoing sweeping structural changes that cut across industry lines, geography, and corporate size.

Top-Down Is Out

Most compnaies have been formally structured from the top down in a strict military or hierarchical model. Upper management sits at the top of a pyramid, with varying layers of middle managers in the middle, and hundreds of supervisors and workers below. Orders issued at the top filter down through the organization. A single group of top individuals makes decisions; influence is top-down.

Flatter and Less Formal Is In

Today, however, the way companies work is becoming less formal and relationships throughout a typical organization are starting to change.

Companies are taking decentralization to its logical conclusion and the corporate structure itself is changing. The layers of middle manangement—the corporate overseers—are being reduced in some companies by, estimates say, as much as 80 percent. In one study of top corporations, those with the best performance records had fewer than four management layers and those with the worst had as many as eight.

OLD HIERARCHICAL STRUCTURES

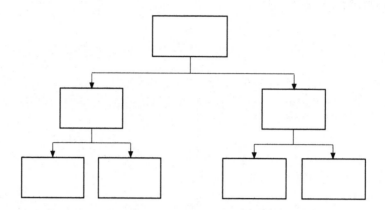

Characterized by:

- Subordinate-boss relationships
- Decisions made at top, executed below
- Management skills: Leadership, planning, controlling, organizing, and integrating people and resources for efficient and effective work production, coaching, counseling, goal and task definition, performance appraisal

Problems solved by:

- Authority
- Procedure
- Management decision

Decisions are:

- Made by single person or with the concensus of a small group of specialists
- Implemented by direction

Relationships are:

- Defined by structure based on loyalty, obedience, leadership

NEW INFLUENCE STRUCTURES

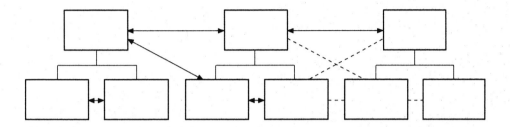

Characterized by:

- Peer, no-authority relationships

- Decisions made by collaboration and involvement

- Management skills: Linking people by being supportive, helpful; sharing power; building trust to serve mutual interests; sharing resources, advice, and aid; performing work efficiently and effectively

Problems solved by:

- Using support and help to establish ground rules for efficiently handling issues

Decisions are:

- Made by sharing power so that alternatives are offered from diverse perspectives and systematically evaluated

- Made by collaboration

Relationships are:

- Based on mutual trust

CAUGHT IN THE MIDDLE

If you're in the middle of an organization you're caught between those above you, whom you are supposed to *serve*, and those below you, whom you must *manage*. In both cases, you must use influence to get the results you want, even though you may not have the organizationally sanctioned power or authority to do so.

So, as a manager or worker, the demands on you are considerable:

- You have to work through others with whom there are often no clear reporting relationships.

- You often have more responsibility than authority.

- There may be no clearly defined goals or criteria for your success.

In this new organizational structure, the way things get done, especially by people in the middle and by staff or ''individual contributors,'' is through influence.

Coercion or formal authority, useful in the old model, no longer works. The influence must be subtle and sincere to get decisions made *upward* with managers, *downward* with subordinates, and *laterally* with peers and coworkers.

Shifts in corporate structures mean we have to work with others without benefit of a clear reporting relationship. Thus we have to influence people over whom we have no formal authority. The way you communicate changes when decisions require support and participation from others who have the resources, skills, and information you need.

PLAYING IT BY EAR

Even though the conditions necessitating good influence skills are likely to emerge in today's business world, in which major structural change is rapidly taking place, you shouldn't eliminate the old management skills from your repertoire. There are clearly certain circumstances that require influence and others that require traditional management.

However, methods must change when decisions require support and participation from others who are outside your sphere of authority; the right method is determined by the situation itself.

Management Skills versus Influence Skills

Management Skills Are Required When:	Influence Skills Are Required When:
Decisions are unilateral.	Decisions require participation and support.
You are in control over people, resources, projects.	Others have expertise, information, contacts, or resources you need to get results.
Issues are simple, predictable, linear.	Issues are complex, unpredictable, nonlinear.
Impact is on single units or departments.	Impact is on multiple units ("ripple effect").
Impact and concerns are narrow, contained.	Organizational impact and concerns are broad.
Results are obtained by controlling, directing, evaluating.	Results are obtained by spontaneity and responsiveness to organizational needs.
Structures are preset.	Structures emerge from assessing issues and setting goals.
You have official recognition.	You need informal support.
You have extrinsic power.	You need intrinsic power.
You work with autonomy.	Success is achieved through interdependence.
The "territory" is defined and contained.	There is territorial overlap.
You are directing.	You are negotiating, persuading.

GETTING AHEAD IN THE AGE OF CHANGE

Changes in the business environment are bringing about another set of radical changes. These are the changes in the way we deal with our careers.

It's Not What You Know

It used to be that when we started up the corporate ladder, we were told that in order to achieve success we simply needed to put in our time and to develop our professional and technical expertise.

It's Not Who You Know

After a while, this began to change and we heard that "it's not what you know, it's who you know". We began to learn the importance of contacts, and how to build a network of helpful people.

So What Is It?

Now we have entered a new era. You can't count on technical or professional expertise alone. These skills can quickly become obsolete. And you simply can't count on your contacts to get what you want. High-level contacts can vanish overnight with the next corporate shake-up, budget cut, acquisition or merger. What you need is something of your own, an inner resource or ability which you can tap whenever it's called for. What you need, in short, is *influence:* a set of people skills that can serve you whenever and wherever you are, a set of interpersonal skills that you can practice anytime, anywhere, inside or outside an organization.

WE CALL IT PORTABLE POWER

YOUR OWN ORGANIZATION

As you go through this book and learn new concepts of influence, think about the people you work with and their relationship to you. Apply the skills directly to these relationships since they are of the most immediate importance to you.

Your Company's Structure

For this exercise, draw a diagram of *your* organization. Make sure to put yourself in the chart.

My Organization

Exercise: What's Your Perspective?

Now that you have drawn a diagram of your organization answer the following questions.

1. What are the underlying forces that have created this structure? Think about the trends in the new work environment. Which of these has had the greatest effect on your company, and why?

   _____

   _____

   _____

   _____

2. Write down the names of three people in the boxes that are connected to yours by whatever lines you drew. Next, ask yourself what are the major differences between you and the people in the adjoining boxes? Do they have more or different skills? More or less power? Write these differences next to each name you wrote.

   _____

   _____

   _____

   _____

3. What do you have in common with these people? Do they have the same skills? Are you on the same level?

   _____

   _____

   _____

   _____

4. Is each of these people resistant to you or receptive to you? If they are resistant to you, state why. Are there power differences? A personallity clash?

   _____

   _____

   _____

   _____

PART

III

How to Influence Anybody

THE FORMULA FOR SUCCESS

INFLUENCE = ATTENTIVENESS + FLEXIBILITY

In other words, the amount of influence you exercise is in direct proportion to how closely you pay attention and how flexible you are. *Attentiveness* is the ability to read another person, situation, and underlying clues. It is a human sonar system—a sensitivity to both verbal and nonverbal communication. In other words, to become a master practitioner of the fine art of listening and observing. *Flexibility* is the ability to shift to an appropriate behavior, depending on how attentive you are to the verbal and nonverbal clues the other person is giving you.

Learning How Best to Apply Influence Skills

The formula above is the foundation of more than just influence. These human skills—flexibility and attentiveness—and their application have their basis in the science of cybernetics. *Cybernetics* is the comparative study of natural systems and systems of mechanical control in order to better understand control and communication in both systems.

In this way, the goals of influence and cybernetics are analogous.

You can think of flexibility this way: If you notice that what you're doing is not giving you the results you want, don't continue those same behaviors harder or longer. Stop, and try another tack.

If you can sense important clues by being attentive and can intepret these clues as a signal to change your behavior, then you'll have a better chance of getting what you want. You have to learn to alter your strategies to the situation and the other person in order to have more influence.

Developing an ability to be flexible is a key concept for effective influencing. In other words, if what you're doing isn't working, don't do it harder or louder or stronger, do something else! Almost anything else will work better than what you're already doing. At first, it will be a matter of trial and error, until you learn what techniques work best in different situations and with different people. But as you practice, you'll soon find that flexibility comes more naturally to you. Flexibility is the key to influence, and is well worth practicing.

Be attentive to what someone is telling you, and be flexible enough to use this information. Remember: **Influence = Attentiveness + Flexibility**. The more attentive you are in recognizing another person's style, the more flexible you'll be in dealing with that person.

LIKE LIKES LIKE

The best way to effect change is first to understand how someone is influenced—which means being attentive to the style of influence the other person is using. Your level of flexibility is seen in your ability to adapt your style to match the other person's communication. Others will feel more comfortable and less defensive if you speak their "language." The other person's "language" means literally the key words they use. These are the verbal clues you have to learn to recognize.

Think back to the list of words that influence you which you were asked to make in the first group of exercises. What words did you list? What style is represented by the words you wrote?

Suppose, for example, that the key word you used was *trust*. That is, the key ingredient that caused you to be influenced was that you trusted the person. Or you may have listed such words as *shared vision* or *brighter future* as being the key elements that influence you. Some people may have reported that they said "yes" when they were on the receiving end of someone's influence attempt because there was a clear *benefit* stated. And that the benefit seemed to zero in on some need or goal that they, the recipient, had.

Word matches reinforce the point that people are usually influenced in the way that they—consciously or unconsciously—influence others.

Most people reveal that the style in which they are influenced is very similar to their own influence style. This fact just reinforces the point that people are usually influenced in the way they—consciously or unconsciously—influence others. Like likes like. It's a basic principle in all Nature.

IV

The Art of Listening:
The Underrated
"Power Tool"

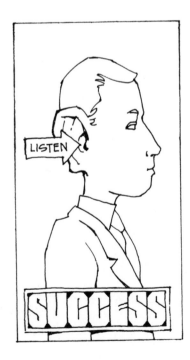

WHY LISTENING IS SO DIFFICULT

Your attitude toward listening is as important as the skill itself.

Listening sounds like such an easy thing to do. All that's required is keeping your mouth shut and your ears open. But *really* keeping our ears open seems to be a herculean task for many of us.

Why?

Distractions

Part of the answer is that we are faced with a multitude of distractions—both internal and external.

Lack of Training

Sometimes, we simply tune out. We seem to enter a mental black hole. The mind of an untrained listener often randomly voyages across a vast uncharted territory of thought while appearing to pay close attention, even to the point of adding such appropriate responses as "really," "yes?" and "uh-huh."

Filtering

Sometimes our inability to listen—to hear what people are actually telling us—occurs because generally we perceive the world in ways that reflect our own needs.

Self-Absorption

Another cause of poor listening skills is our preoccupation with our own agenda. While the other person is speaking we are busy planning what we want to say and mentally rehearsing our responses.

Developing new attitudes and approaches toward listening—and practicing them—are the "power tools" of influence.

HOW WELL DO YOU LISTEN?

LISTENING TO INFLUENCE

1. Listening without Judging

The Japanese symbol for the word "listen" is composed of the character for "ear" placed within the character for "gate." This pictograph makes sense. When we listen to someone, we are, in effect, passing through the other person's gate and entering his world.

When we are really listening we are receiving the other person's attitudes in an open, nonjudgmental way. Being so open-minded can be risky because the speaker's point of view may challenge our own. It takes courage, but it is worthwhile because to listen well is to view the world from another person's vantage point.

To listen in a truly open, nonjudgmental way requires a lot of inner security. Most of us are afraid to listen in this way because we believe that we might be *changed*, that our beliefs may be altered or that we may lose our identity.

But all that's required to listen in this way is *acceptance* not necessarily *agreement*. Even if you really hear another person out, you can always return to your own beliefs and opinions. But first, you must listen with an open mind.

If someone senses through your verbal and nonverbal behavior that you are listening openly and acceptingly, that person will feel far less threatened by you and be much more open. Lines of defense drop; consequently, he or she will feel freer to explore other angles or options—and will be much more receptive to what *you* have to say.

By listening to another person openly, you convey a forceful message. You say: "I'm interested in you as a person, and I think what you have to say is important. I'm not trying to judge or evaluate you. I respect your thoughts, and even if I don't agree with them, I know that they are valid for you."

When you practice this sort of listening, you'll find attitudes and behavior are contagious. If you listen actively and respectfully, chances are that you will be *listened to* respectfully when it's your turn to speak.

2. Developing a Genuine Interest in Others

Really listening to others requires an attitude of sincere interest and curiosity and *an honest desire to see things the way another person sees them*. It requires that you temporarily suspend judgment—that for the moment you ignore yourself and your attachment to your own ideas.

For instance, imagine that you're visiting another planet and the individual with whom you are speaking is an intelligent being you have discovered there. Simply gather information. What does the extraterrestrial look like, sound like? What does she talk about? Remember—don't evaluate what you perceive, and don't judge it, even to yourself as good, bad, stupid, smart, or silly. Just observe.

Once you've trained yourself to listen in this way you'll see and hear things you would have overlooked before. You may find that people are more intriguing or interesting to you. Ignore your urge to decide whether you like them, whether they are like you, or whether they fit into your frame of reference. If you can suspend judgement, you're apt to discover a better sense of rapport with others.

3. Learning to Ask Good Questions

Sometimes even when you want to know more about another person, you may hesitate to ask questions because you don't want to, fearing that it seems nosy. Usually, however, the contrary is true. Most people feel complimented when they are asked questions—they are flattered that someone is expressing interest in them.

The first key to asking good questions is *tuning into your own curiosity*. What do *you* want to know about this person? Once you know *what* you want to ask, use the following tips to get clear, informative answers:

- *Ask open-ended questions:* A shy or reticent person may take the easy way out if your inquiries can be answered with a simple yes or no. For example, instead of "Did you regret making that decision?," ask "How did you feel about making that decision?"

- *Create cycles of learning:* Use some facet of the person's answer to your previous question as a springboard to your next question: "Can you tell me more about why you decided to launch your own company?"

- *Ask for more detail:* Most people speak in generalities. The way to get more interesting, "meaty" information from them is to ask for more detail: "What specifically do you wish you could have done differently?"

- *Avoid turn-off questions:* "How" or "what" questions are usually better received than "why" questions. People often feel defensive when asked to explain their motivations ("why" questions). Often they haven't thought through their reasons or they don't wish to disclose them.

When you ask people *how* they did something, your interest in the process by which they accomplished something is flattering to them. You will also sometimes get an interesting inside look at their modus operandi (m.o.)—their way of doing things—which can help you in influencing them.

Here are a few general questions that can help get people talking:

- "What's your understanding of this situation?"

- "What are your goals for this project? What outcome are you looking for?"

- "I'm wondering . . . I'm curious about . . ."

- "How did you arrive at that decision?" or "What were the most important criteria for you in making that decision?" (These questions offer you a glimpse of their decision-making strategies, which can be useful for evaluating their capabilities in a particular area.)

- "What caused you to . . . ?" or "What motivated you to . . . ?" (Here, you're looking to underlying reasons, motivations, and catalysts to people's decision making.)

4. Developing the Art of Helping with Silence

Many people believe that just listening without injecting comments or advice seems too passive or compliant. It is a curious and unfortunate aspect of our culture that we tend to think that any action is better than no action, and that just listening or absorbing means you're a wimp, a procrastinator, or a do-nothing.

Jack Gibb, an early figure of humanistic psychology, often says "help isn't always helpful." What he means is that, even with the best intentions, we are often too directive. We tell others what they should or shouldn't do or what worked for us. While we feel helpful, we may not help others to arrive at the best solution for them. Neither do we empower them to stand on their own two feet and come up with their own solutions. Advice and information are usually seen rightly as attempts to change a person. They serve as barriers to self-expression. Ultimately the advice is seldom taken and the information is discarded.

Suppose someone in your life—your boss, a colleague, your spouse, or a friend—is telling you about a difficult situation he or she is in. Your simple task is just to listen, *without* doing all the other, non-pure listening things we all do. For example, try not to jump in and tell them about a similar situation you encountered once and how you solved your problem. And try not to refer them to some sources where they can find advice or help (until you've first listened to what they have to say). All your recommendations might be useful and well-meaning in their place, but by adding and intervening, you are not simply "being there" for the other person. And often, when people are having troubles or difficulty, all they really want is someone to simply listen. Chances are, your troubled friend, colleague, or relative knows the solution or can figure it out. What he or she needs, though, is someone just to be there, like a mirror.

5. Developing a Desire to Accommodate

Why be accommodating when you're trying to get people to think or do things your way?

Accommodation can be a key factor in softening someone's resistance. In a study of negotiations, it was found that the most successful bargaining sessions occur when one party offers a few concessions (accommodations) early in the game. By offering concessions, people change the environment and are able to get more of what they wanted in the long run.

Sometimes we have to give up "being right" in the ultimate service of "winning."

What this means is that sometimes we have to give up "being right" in the ultimate service of "winning." If you argue or try to talk people out of their needs and wants, you may score a point here or there, but you will probably not gain much in the way of trust. Nor will you make much progress in building a strong long-term relationship.

This doesn't mean you should approach a negotiation as though you're giving up everything you want. What's important is an *attitude* of willingness to consider the other person's point of view and a willingness to make a few concessions if necessary. In this way you can best achieve your ultimate goals.

Accommodation Quick-Check

Check the items that apply to you.

☐ I am interested in the needs of the other person.

☐ A win-win situation is my preferred outcome.

☐ I am a good listener.

☐ I am willing to give up something to get something.

☐ I know what I want to accomplish.

6. Practice Makes Perfect

OPEN LISTENING

Simply practice listening; that is, apply yourself to hearing what you are being told—try to be "all ears." One way to check yourself to see whether you're really hearing what you're being told is to observe, as you are listening, where your mind is going and what you are thinking about.

Try to eliminate some of the "noise" going on simultaneously in your mind by concentrating more on the other person, and then see what happens to the quality of your conversation.

ACTIVE LISTENING

Another kind of listening, which is a little more proactive, is called *active listening.* An active listener "restates" the content of what is being said. This means putting into your own words the meaning of what has just been said. You must be careful, though, not to use their words to express *your* thoughts so that you change the essential meaning. Simply try to clarify the phrase or sentence, without changing the basic integrity of what has been said.

Try to echo, in words, what the person is saying. Suppose your friend says to you, "My boss is really giving me a hard time today." You can restate this by responding, "Sounds like your boss is on your case for some reason." For this kind of listening, the simplest kind, you can echo simply to check whether you "got" the communication the way the other person sent it.

ENCOURAGE PRECISE COMMUNICATION

42

REFLECTING FEELINGS

Another active listening techniques is called *reflecting feelings*. This technique is similar to restating in that you attempt to mirror back what you hear. However, instead of restating the ideas, you try to reflect the feelings or emotion behind them. For example, if someone says to you, "My friends always ask me to do favors for them as though they think I have all the time in the world on my hands." If you were to reflect the feelings of this statement, you might say, "You sound angry about that." Here, you are listening for the tone expressed by the spoken words.

Caution: When reflecting feelings, you are, at best, only *guessing* at the feelings the person may be having. So, you may want to try a few different feeling statements, "You sound like you're feeling overwhelmed and frustrated." Then, the other person has the chance to let you know whether your sense of the emotion they have is acually the correct one.

OPEN-ENDED QUESTIONING

Another active listening technique involves using *open-ended questions*. These are the kinds of questions that do not easily lend themselves to simple "yes" or "no" answers. Usually they begin with *what, why,* or *how.* For example, "What do you think you can do about the person?" "How can your friends learn to be more sensitive to you?" Try answering those with a simple yes or no! Open-ended questions are a great way to get a person to open up and share with you.

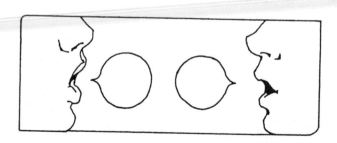

Exercise: The Art of Listening

The following exercises test your use of the new listening techniques.

Use a specific situation with a person you're trying to influence. Use only *one* of these listening techniques at a time until you've had a chance to practice and develop some skills.

1. Open Listening

Listen to exactly what the person is saying. Do not add, edit or interpret their statements. Write down exactly what you heard, one sentence at a time. Then, show it to the person you listened to and ask him/her for feedback on how accurately you captured and heard what they said. The person said:

_____

_____

_____

Write down all the "noise" you hear in your mind, in addition to what you're listening to, from the other person. Once you start noticing this, you can train yourself to edit or screen this out. The extra "noise" I added:

_____

_____

_____

2. Active Listening

Your restatement of what the person said (put it into your own words, being careful not to interpret, analyze, add to or subtract from what they said). Just clarify:

_____

_____

_____

44

Exercise (continued)

3. Reflecting Feelings
Your "guess" of what the person might be feeling:

_____

_____

_____

4. Open-ended Questions
This is your attempt to gather more information than they gave in their first communication. Write your question and then the answer you get.

What? Q: _____

A: _____

How? Q: _____

A: _____

When?Q: _____

A: _____

Why? Q: _____

A: _____

Who? Q: _____

A: _____

BLOCK-BUSTING QUESTIONS

Block-busting questions offer another way to elicit more precise communication from another person by eliminating ambiguities.

Here's a simple illustration: Take the statement, "Let's work out an agenda." If someone said this to you in a work context, what would it mean? You might understand this as a project and go back to your workspace, *thinking* you knew what the other person meant but not being sure. Then, you'd scratch your head and try to work out an agenda according to what you thought the person meant. But unless you checked it out, you could be way off base. What does *agenda* mean to that person? Does it mean the list of events, the speakers, a detailed, step-by-step plan for the meeting, or just an overall outline? What is meant by *work out*, and who is going to be responsible for it?

There are various ways to frame questions to get the other person to be more specific. You can ask, "What, specifically, do you mean by . . .?" Or, "Can you give me some more information?" Or, "I wonder if you could give me an example of an agenda that worked well at your last meeting?" Or, "What information would you like included in the agenda?" Usually people speak in generalities and they believe the listener knows clearly what they mean. Asking block-busting questions breaks through to the true meaning and gets you the more precise, more specific information you need.

Exercise: Rephrasing for Clarification

For each of the statements below, ask yourself block-busting questions until you get more specific meaning and understanding of the sentence. Write (a) the block-busting questions you used and (b) the expanded, fuller statements that your questions elicit.

Example Questions

1. "Let's work out the agenda.

   a. Block-busting question:

   Ex. What specifically do you mean by *agenda*?

   b. Revised statement:

   Ex. The list of events for the meeting.

   a. Block-busting question:

   Ex. What events?

   b. Revised statement:

   Ex. The stress management workshops.

   a. Block-busting question:

   _____

   b. Revised statement:

   _____

2. "I want to get *that* out today."

   a. Block-busting question:

   _____

   b. Revised statement:

   _____

   a. Block-busting question:

   _____

   b. Revised Statement:

   _____

3. "Training should cover most of the policy procedures."

   a. Block-busting question:

   _____

   b. Revised statement:

   _____

   a. Block-busting question:

   _____

   b. Revised Statement:

   _____

   a. Block-busting question:

   _____

   b. Revised statement:

   _____

4. "Higher visibility will get us the notice we want."

   a. Block-busting question:

   _____

   b. Revised statement:

   _____

   a. Block-busting question:

   _____

   b. Revised statement:

   _____

   a. Block-busting question:

   _____

   b. Revised statement:

   _____

Exercise (continued)

5. "We need to plan for anticipated growth."

   a. Block-busting question:

   _____

   b. Revised statement:

   _____

   a. Block-busting question:

   _____

   b. Revised statement:

   _____

   a. Block-busting question:

   _____

   b. Revised statement:

   _____

COMPARATORS: PRECISION QUESTIONS

Precision questions help get a clearer understanding of what the person means when he or she uses comparators. Precision listening leads to precision questions. *Comparators* are words and phrases used to compare one idea to another. Often, comparators are imprecise and unclear. For example, your boss may tell you to be "more productive." Well, what specifically does that mean? More productive than what? Than you were last year? Last month? More productive than your coworkers?

You may respond to these statements by asking, "How do *you measure* productivity?" or "More productive compared to what, or who?" If you ask these questions directly, and in a way that indicates that you are seeking a better, clearer understanding, you will not seem to be challenging or threatening to the other person.

Qualifying Comparators

The following statements are called *comparators*, which are often used when comparing one idea to another. To avoid possible misinterpretation and get more precise information, statements like these must be qualified. Try your hand at qualifying the statements below to get clearer communication. Here are a couple of examples to get you started:

Comparator: That's a better way to do it.

Qualifying question: On what basis do you consider it better?

Comparator: We've had very good profits this year.

Qualifying question: When you say "good," what are you comparing it to?

Exercise: Clarifying Communications

Rewrite the statements to clarify the meaning.

1. *That's a better way to do it.*

   a. Qualifier: Ex. Better than what? _____

   b. Qualifier: Ex. What do you mean by *better*? _____

2. *We've had very good profits this year.*

   a. Qualifier: What do you mean by *good*? _____

   b. Qualifier: _____

3. *I have a better idea.*

   a. Qualifier: _____

   b. Qualifier: _____

4. *Doing it this way requires less effort.*

   a. Qualifier: _____

   b. Qualifier: _____

5. *We should set higher standards.*

   a. Qualifier: _____

   b. Qualifier: _____

UNIVERSALS

Another category of imprecise statements you may hear are *universals*, statements that declare that something is absolutely true or false. The way you can tell when people are using a universal is when they use the words *always, never, all,* or *none*. This indicates a black-or-white mode of thinking that often leads to hasty generalizations. In order to practice precision, you can ask simple block-busting questions, such as "How do you know all _____ are lazy?" or simply "All?" Such questions challenge the notion that what is claimed is always and forever true. You might also ask, "Can you think of a time when this was not the case?" thereby challenging the other person to question his or her own absolute thinking.

If people took the time to ask a few simple clarifying questions, they would be equipped to be powerful listeners and better influencers.

Qualifying Universal Statements

For each of the statements below, write a few precision questions that might get the person to state the point more specifically. Then, write a revised statement you would like to elicit as a result of your question.

1. Each supervisor is responsible for her entire department.

   a. Qualifier: Ex. The *entire* department? _____ ?

   b. More accurate revision:

      Ex. All the supervisory and hourly staff. _____

2. All management is concerned with its profits.

   a. Qualifier: _____ ?

   b. More accurate revision:

      _____

3. Everyone here supports one another.

   a. Qualifier: _____ ?

   b. More accurate revision:

      _____

Exercise (continued)

4. My supervisor never notices the extra work I do.

   a. Qualifier: _____ ?

   b. More accurate revision:

   _____

5. Nobody shows me any respect.

   a. Qualifier: _____ ?

   b. More accurate revision:

   _____

6. Everyone does the easiest thing.

   a. Qualifier: _____ ?

   b. More accurate revision:

   _____

7. No one can do my job but me.

   a. Qualifier: _____ ?

   b. More accurate revision:

   _____

8. My manager doesn't trust anyone.

   a. Qualifier: _____ ?

   b. More accurate revision:

   _____

9. I can tell you every response she'll make.

   a. Qualifier: _____ ?

   b. More accurate revision:

   _____

10. We can't ever get what we need from the support staff.

    a. Qualifier: _____ ?

    b. More accurate revision:

    _____

PART

V

Refined Listening

FINE-TUNING YOUR RADAR

Any successful salesperson knows that no matter how great the product, it's not going to sell unless the buyer has a need for it. That need may be real (Mark *needs* a new coat because his has holes in it) or it may be perceived (Mark *needs* a new coat because he thinks his is out of style). And, of course, the good salesperson doesn't wait for the buyer to recognize his or her own need. The skilled seller is alert to the subtle cues that signal a customer's true needs, and then uses the cues to demonstrate how a particular item addresses those needs. How does the seller discover the buyer's needs? Through careful listening.

There are really only two times when most of us listen extremely well.

1. When something truly interests us. Even then our ability to listen can be negatively affected, for example, if we're preoccupied with a problem.

2. When we know we must. In these situations we generally need to get specific information—answers to questions such as ''How do I get to the highway from here?'' or ''Doctor, what do the test results mean?''

In order to be skilled at influencing others, it's important to master the ability to listen effectively in a broad range of situations. Then you'll be able to tune in to others when it's important to you—and when it's important to them. This is done through the process of *refined listening*—listening on a more subtle level and focusing on the more elusive elements of communication.

There are three important parts of refined listening:

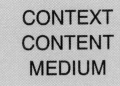

THE CONTEXT

The context of a communication includes both the external and internal environment of the interaction.

The External Environment

The external environment is the physical setting where the communication takes place—your office, someone else's office, a neutral work environment like a conference room, or a social setting like a restaurant. Whenever a conversation takes place on one person's turf, that person has a decided advantage in negotiation. That's because he or she feels more comfortable in that environment. If you are on neutral territory, then all things being equal, you will interact on a more equal basis.

The Internal Environment

The internal environment is the *circumstance* of your communication with another person.

- What emotional or intellectual factors are affecting each of you?
- What is going on in your lives at that time?
- What is the emotional setting?
- Is the other person tense or relaxed, feeling secure or shaky, depressed or elated over, say, a recent promotion?
- What is your relationship with the person?
- Is he above or below you in the organizational hierarchy?
- Is this a one-time encounter or an ongoing relationship?
- Is he responding with his own authority or ideas, or is he being influenced by others or by company rules or policies?

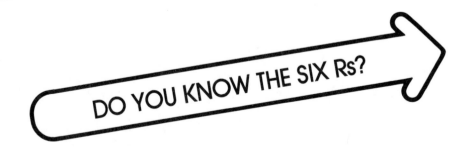
DO YOU KNOW THE SIX Rs?

THE SIX Rs

In any conversation, evaluate the internal context of the situation. It is easier with people whom you know well, but it can also be done with people you've only just met. There are six variables to consider. Together they form the six Rs:

1. Relationship

Ask yourself: What is the nature of your relationship?
Have you worked together before or are you strangers? Is it strictly business or do you also have a personal friendship?

To gauge a relationship, measure these two components: longevity and intensity. For longevity, consider not only how long you've already worked with (or interacted with) this person, but also how long you expect to work with him or her in the future.

To measure intensity, consider the depth of your relationship. Is it a superficial, nodding acquaintanceship? Or is it a close relationship in which you will be working together as a team or as part of a task force over a given period of time?

2. Range

What is the range of the other person's authority or responsibility in your discussion and in the organization as a whole? What is the range of his or her network of contacts within and outside of the organization?

3. Record

What is the other person's history of response to you? What does this person's record for accepting new ideas or proposals reveal? Begin with whatever background information you can gather, and then make your own evidence-based judgment.

4. Reasons

It's important to be aware of each party's reasons for communicating. To understand a person's motivations you may have to do a bit of guesswork, especially if you're in a situation where you don't know the person well. And you may have to begin with some probing and questioning to uncover what his or her real reasons and motivations are.

5. Rules

Rules are our limits or boundaries. Rules are often expressed in statements that contain words such as *should, shouldn't, must, mustn't, have to, can't, always,* and *never.* It's important to be aware of the rules of others, whether they are actually valid or exist only in that person's head. If the rules a person adheres to are valid, they may be related to company policy, precedent, professional norms, or ethics. If ceratin rules are valid to only one person, they are constraints that the person believes to exist.

It's not your job to judge these rules or the person who follows them. Your only task is to listen and to be aware that personal rules represent restrictions and boundaries for that person's behavior.

6. Resistance

Resistance is very common in both selling and influencing. If you're lucky, you get a foot-dragging response, but not an out-and-out no. A resistance statement, such as "I'm not sure yet," "We've never done this before," or "We don't have enough time (or money)," usually means that the person is asking for something from you. It could be more information about what you're proposing, reassurance that he is not making a mistake, or more rewards or benefits that will be gained from saying yes to you.

Effective influencers realize that resistance is a natural part of the influence process. In fact, they welcome it as an important and necessary step in the process.

Exercise: The Six Rs

1. **Relationship**
   How long have I known the person? _____
   Have we worked together before? _____
   On a team? _____ As a boss/subordinate? _____
   As a colleague? _____
   Is the relationship strictly business? _____
   Do we have a personal friendship? _____
   Do we have things, people, projects in common? _____

2. **Range**
   Range of your authority? _____
   Range of other person's authority? _____
   Range of their network inside and outside of the organization? _____
   _____

3. **Record**
   His/her response to you in the past? _____
   How have they accepted new ideas before? _____

4. **Reasons**
   Theirs: _____
   Yours: _____

5. **Rules**
   Rules, real and imaginary, you have heard from the person: _____
   _____
   Should? _____
   Should not? _____
   Have to? _____
   Can't _____
   Always? _____
   Never? _____

6. **Resistance**
   Statements of resistance you have *already* heard in this situation or are anticipating
   will come up: _____
   _____

Content
Write a brief summary of your version of the content in this situation. Try to
pare it down to "just the facts" without extraneous information.

_____
_____
_____
_____
_____

THE CONTENT

Content is the substance of the message—what the person is talking about. *It is made up of all the words, facts, and ideas in a communication.*

With a few straight-shooting people, the content of the message is all there is— they say exactly what they mean. You probably know one or two of these brutally honest people. Some even preface their remarks with ''I'm going to level with you . . . ,'' and what you get from them is a direct opinion on the matter you're discussing.

Too often however, we act as if content is all there is in our interactions with people. This can sometimes be deceptive because content alone does not usually convey the speaker's entire message.

Depending on the *context*, a story's *content* will take on different meanings. If you talk about a new business idea, a colleague may use this story to encourage you to move ahead. If you discern from the context that he has been feeling dissatisfied with his job, his content may be his way of hinting to you about his own hopes for the future.

CONTENT   CONTEXT

COMMUNICATION

THE MEDIUM

The medium is the packaging of communication. It provides the richest area for refined listeners, for it is here that you often get the most valuable information. The external package of a message often has more impact than the message itself. In other words, *how* you are told something is as important as the message itself.

Refined Listening

Bookstores are filled with books on body language. Most of them indicate that a clenched jaw signifies anger, crossing the arms is supposed to convey disinterest or boredom, and blushing means embarrassment. The danger in interpreting these signals is generalizing too much. A clenched jaw may not always mean anger. It may indicate stress or a jaw condition. Blushing may not indicate embarrassment. It may signal frustration or anger.

Most of us are not trained to notice small bits of behavior unless they produce large changes, and we often misinterpret the changes we do see—a clenched jaw or crossed arms for example. We ascribe meaning to what we see based on our own use of these gestures or our past experiences with others.

You can begin training yourself to notice physiological changes. But don't generalize. Keep your observations specific to each person you're interacting with. If there are five people at a meeting, you may see five different sets of encoded, nonverbal behavior. What may seem like the same nonverbal response in two people may signal something very different about each person's internal state. Just notice and observe. Do not try to interpret or attribute any meaning to what you see.

NONVERBAL COMMUNICATIONS

TUNING IN TO WHAT'S UNSPOKEN

Body language can even be *more* indicative of a person's true state than the spoken word. There are several categories of nonverbal, unconscious, physiological responses that people exhibit and that you can look for. Usually these are actions outside of a person's conscious awareness. Here are some of the most important and easily visible ones:

1. Body Posture and Gestures

These body signals include:

- Sudden straightness of the spine
- Position of the head
- Position of the feet on the floor
- Distribution of weight on hips and lower legs
- Hand movements and gestures

As an experiment, the next time you're having a conversation with someone you know well, note as many of these signals as you can. At different times you may see the person's weight shift, moving from one leg to the other. For this individual, this posturing may indicate a change of mood or internal state—though for another person, it may indicate something else.

Make a friend or colleague your research population of one. Watch nonverbal signals closely. After you practice, it will be difficult for your subject to fool you, despite the words being spoken. You will have gathered indisputable evidence of what the person's body does outside of his or her conscious control or awareness. Similarly, you can discover when a person is feeling supportive, interested, bored, disagreeable, or in some other mood.

It is critical that your observations be descriptive, not evaluative. Your initial mental or written note should be "left leg weight shift," not "George seems nervous." In time, you'll begin to associate a particular posture or gesture with its corresponding internal state. There are more subtle but also easily detectable changes that you'll pick up once you begin noticing them.

2. Skin Color Changes

If you watch carefully, you can begin to see different colorations in a person's face at different times. For example, note the contrast between nose color and the skin color of the forehead. Blushes, of course, are easy to spot, but a blush isn't always in the cheeks. There are different types of blushes. Watch for them:

- At the tip of the ears
- On the forehead
- At the jawline

The blush may be rosy and soft, a purply pink all over the face, or blotchy red. Some people blush when they're embarrassed, some when they're angry, others when presented with a challenge, still others when they're sexually excited. Again, your purpose as a refined listener is not to assign judgment, but just to observe these changes in any given person.

3. Minute Muscle Changes

Small muscle changes are idiosyncratic. Like other physiological responses, they vary widely from person to person. Watch for:

- Muscle tightness or slackness near the edges of the mouth
- Tightness or squinting around the eyes
- Tightness at the jaw line
- The formation of creases on the forehead or directly between the eyes

4. Lower Lip Changes

These are the most common of the small muscle changes. Sometimes when people are feeling pressured or uncomfortable, their lower lip tenses. That's where expressions like *tight-lipped* come from. Some people seem to be this way all the time, but upon closer observation, you'll see that their lips are tighter at some times than at others.

Of course, tightness is not the only kind of lip change. Others include:

- Fullness
- Movement
- Size
- Shape
- Color
- Wetness
- Dryness
- Trembling
- Texture (smooth or rough)

5. Breathing Changes

Changes in breathing are an early barometer of someone's mood. The easiest way to observe a person's breathing rate is to watch the up-and-down movement of their chest or abdomen. Sometimes you can even pick up signals by watching the shadow of a person's shoulder against a background wall. You can see the pattern of rising and falling with every breath.

Rapid breathing will only mean something about someone's internal state if you've watched them often enough or long enough to know how they breathe when they're excited and when they're calm.

6. Voice Patterns: Tone, Tempo and Volume

Voices have a number of characteristics, any one of which can vary. The tone can be high or low, loud or soft. The tempo can be fast or slow, with certain pauses or without them. The volume can be smooth or variable, booming or cooing. Some voices squeak, other voices sing. Again, try not to evaluate what you hear. Notice the range of possibilities and variations in voice among different people and within the same person at different times.

Because there is no visual distraction, telephone conversations offer an excellent opportunity to practice developing your sensitivity to voice changes. To begin, notice just *one* of the dimensions of voice quality: the tone, the volume, or the speed. With practice, you can acquire a sensitivity to all of them.

Don't make assumptions about what changes in voice mean. Simply note the changes. When you've gathered enough examples of how someone's voice alters when they're angry, or how it changes when they are confused, then you can test your assumptions by asking them, "How are you feeling about this idea?"

If you can develop this sensory acuity, you can use your finely tuned radar to notice things that most other people do not. You can be a living lie detector and a powerful influencer.

REPRESENTATIONAL SYSTEMS

Another useful way to refine your listening is to listen for which of the five senses—sight, sound, touch, smell, or taste—a person depends upon regularly as a channel through which to perceive the world, process information, and communicate. Some people, for example, experience life as a series of moving or still pictures. Others focus on sounds, such as voices, music, and noise, as a way to "see" the world. They may remember the words they have heard or their own internal voices. Still others experience life primarily through touching and other bodily sensations.

Each of us has a preferred sensory channel. If you listen, you will hear people actually *telling* you which one they prefer. They will use certain language and figures of speech which, in effect, tell you something about how their minds work.

A VISUAL PERSON

Uses phrases like "That's the way I see it," "It seems clear to me," or "Let's watch this carefully."

AN AUDITORY PERSON

Says "I hear what you're saying," "That rings a bell," or "It doesn't sound right to me."

A KINESTHETIC PERSON

Uses physical or tactile images. His or her language will include expressions like "I'm getting a grasp on the situation," "When the new policy takes hold . . . ," or "It feels right to me."

A GUSTATORY PERSON

Uses phrases such as "It leaves a good taste in my mouth," "I need to chew on it for a while," or "That's a spicy idea."

AN OLFACTORY PERSON

Says "It didn't smell right to me," "This deal smells fishy," or "She came out of it smelling like a rose."

By listening for statements like these and learning how to read them, you are on the way to acquiring the fortune teller's craft. It's an important influence skill.

Exercise: Practice Refined Listening

Nonverbal Repsonse Inventory

As you are listening, make notes on your observations of the body language—movements, postures and gestures—the other person is expressing. Remember to be descriptive, not valuative.

Position of head: _____

Position of feet: _____

Distribution of weight on hips and lower legs: _____

Hand movements and gestures: _____

Skin color changes: _____

Small muscle changes:

   edges of mouth _____

   around corner of eyes: _____

   jaw lines: _____

   forehead: _____

   lower lip: _____

Breathing changes:

   slow/quick: _____

   rhythmic/uneven: _____

Voice patterns:

   tone: _____

   tempo: _____

   volume: _____

Representational Systems

Make notes, as you listen, on the ''sensory channels'' the person is referring to as you hear their phrases and words:

Visual (words/phrases/clues): _____

Auditory (words/phrases/clues): _____

Kinesthetic (words/phrases/clues): _____

Gustatory (words/phrases/clues): _____

Olfactory (words/phrases/clues): _____

PART

VI

The Magic of Rapport

SETTING THE STAGE FOR GREATER INFLUENCE

RAPPORT

This is the feeling of trust and comfort we have when we're with someone who knows, hears, understands, accepts, and values us. Some people call it chemistry. It is usually the result of a close association between two people who have shared experiences or who share a common philosophy or background. Sometimes rapport comes quickly—often because of shared interests or perhaps because a person reminds you of someone with whom you already have rapport—but usually it takes years to develop.

Rapport is the foundation of most of our relationships. Without it, no matter how much we may like or respect another person, we feel distant, removed, or out-of-sync with people for whom we may otherwise have high regard or respect. With it, we may disagree or see some things differently, but we still feel that we basically have a connection, an identifiable bond, with someone else—sometimes with people we have very little in common with.

ENTRAINMENT

This is the basis for rapport. It is a process whereby two or more units become synchronized. If you use entrainment, you'll find that you can establish rapport with almost anyone, even people with whom you never thought you could connect.

INFLUENCE = ATTENTIVENESS + FLEXIBILITY

ENTRAINMENT AND THE RHYTHM OF RAPPORT

The phenomenon of rapport, it turns out, is universal. Whenever two or more oscillators in the same field pulse at *nearly* the same time, they tend to lock in so that they pulse at *exactly* the same time. Why?

Scientists have concluded that nature seeks the most efficient energy state, and it apparently takes less energy to pulse in cooperation than in opposition.

Sympathetic resonance is another term for rapport, relating it to music. Humans also have the capacity for sympathetic resonance. There seems to be some sort of a hold mechanism that takes place between two people in conversation, in the words of Dr. William Condon, a *conversational dance*.

Communication is thus like a dance, with everyone engaged in intricate and shared movements across many subtle dimensions, yet all strangely oblivious to what they are doing. Even total strangers display this synchronization. A listener usually does not move as much as a speaker. There are moments when he or she remains quite still. If the listener does move, however, the movements will tend to be synchronous with the speaker's activity. Dr. Condon's conclusion is the more you move in rhythm with someone, the closer you become with that person.

Even when pairs or groups start out aggressively toward one another, a shift in rhythms can sometimes occur.

There are many examples of this sort of entrainment, of matching rhythm, all around us.

- A baby's heartbeat synchronizes with that of its mother.
- A powerful public speaker causes the hearts of listeners to beat in rhythm with his.
- Members of an orchestra, all playing different instruments, move, indeed almost breathe, as one.
- Synchonized heartbeats have been reported between psychiartist and patient.
- Female housemates sometimes find their menstrual cycles synchronized.
- Physical activities such as singing, rowing, or even marching synchronize the breathing of everyone in the group.

ENTRAINMENT AS RAPPORT—
THE HEARTBEAT OF INFLUENCE

When you want to establish rapport with someone, regardless of whether or not you agree with the content of his or her communication, the most expeditious and effective way is consciously to seek entrainment with that person.

First, practice refined listening. Then match, pace, or mirror one or more of the unconscious rhythms or gestures of the other person. Keep to the basic principle of the formula for success: **Influence = Attentiveness** (refined listening) + **Flexibility** (altering your habits to match or mirror what you've seen or heard the other person say or do).

Matching and pacing your rhythms with those of another person are at the heart of influence. Alter your habits to match and pace what you see the other person doing, and echo the voice, tone, and tempo the other person uses. This will enable you to use the different styles of influence with the best results.

Regardless of the subject matter or form with which you intend to match, mirror, or pace, and lead, the principle is always the same:

1. Join people where they are.

2. Establish rapport.

Once you're in tune with them, they're far more likely to respond to you and your efforts to influence them.

Remember, when you are trying to establish instant rapport through entrainment, you must do it in a subtle way so that it's not noticed; otherwise, the people you ultimately want to influence will think (rightly so) that you are mimicking them.

Breaking Rapport

At times it may be appropriate to *break* rapport in order to disengage from a conversation. How do you do this? The easiest way is to *mis*match; that is, when the other person does a particular gesture, instead of matching it, you do something else. One sure way is to look at your watch, or break eye contact, or stand up when the other is sitting. You can also increase your distance from the other person or make an abrupt, unexpected movement.

Matching Breathing

Observation is the first step in matching breathing. Begin by noticing the pattern, pace, and rhythm of the other person's breathing. People breathe high in the chest, or low, or deep in the abdomen. While they're speaking, they breathe fast or slow, with or without pauses. You can gauge someone's breathing by observing the rise or fall of the person's shoulders or the pulse points in the neck or chest.

Then check your own breathing and see which elements (speed, rhythm) are the same or different. Try to synchronize or match *one element at a time*. You may notice, for example, that the person is breathing quite slowly. If your breathing pattern is quick, slow it down until it matches the speed of the other person's. Pretty soon you'll be able to match more than one element, and you'll be breathing in sync with the other person. He or she will feel it, too.

Matching Voice

In business, the easiest and most successful matching technique involves voice. You can match the other person's speed or volume or intonation. You must do this with some subtlety, however, or you run the risk that people will think you're mimicking them. And you shouldn't do it with such precision that it sounds foreign and radically different from your own speech pattern.

Mirroring Movements and Gestures

Imagine you are meeting an influential client in his office. You want to attain an initial rapport before trying to influence this person. You sit in a chair, and place a folder across your lap. He sits rather stiffly and upright in his desk chair. His hands move constantly, straightening out papers on his desk. Of course, you can't pace his hand movements since you don't have any papers to shift. But you can sit just as stiffly without being in exactly the same position. And you don't want to react immediately; if you do, it will look as if you're mimicking him. As your conversation progresses, work to pace his actions and vocal tone.

In this situation, here's how the pacing and matching would work.

- *He leans across the desk toward you.*
  You lean slightly toward him.

- *He leans back in his chair.*
  You lean back to your original position.

- *Soon, his hands stop moving around. He folds them in front of him.*

  You, of course, had your hands that way, on top of a folder in your lap. He's now mirroring you! You now have built a good foundation of rapport by speaking the same body language.

But don't expect cues to be immediate. Entrainment happens over the course of a long conversation, so be observant and patient. Remember, too, that you want to approximate these behaviors, not mimic them. There's a fine line between emulation and mimicry.

Mirroring with Words

When you have observed and listened to another person and discovered that his or her primary mode of experiencing is, say, visual, then the best way to gain rapport is to speak the same language. Match, as well as you can, your mode of expression to that person's mode. Put your questions in language that appeals to the visual: "Can you *see* yourself owning this?" or "Shall I *show* you how it works?" You can also show visuals —graphs, charts, drawings—to a visual person. Simply telling the person something may not be enough.

Similarly, if someone uses an auditory mode of expression, package your communication with auditory-based language: "How does this *sound* to you?"; "Do you think this idea has the right *tone*?"; or "Will this *ring a bell* with management?"

If it's not readily apparent which form of communication a person prefers, you may have to use the trial-and-error approach. If you don't get a response at first, switch to another mode. If the auditory doesn't work, try the kinesthetic: "How does this *feel* to you?" or "Let's *touch base* so we can get a *firm grasp* on the project."

Form as Content

Often, what's most important is not so much the content of what you present, but the language you use to convey it—not *what* you communicate, but *how* you communicate it. Mirroring with words is an important way to establish the instant rapport you need in order to maximize your influence.

LEADING THE WAY

Establishing rapport, though, is just the beginning. Once in sync, a person is likely to follow you. When this role reversal occurs, you know you've gained rapport and can start to use that rapport to gain influence. This step is called *leading*.

Remember, pacing is simply doing something similar to the other person in any of the ways discussed here: matching breathing and voice, mirroring gestures, voice tone, posture, and language style. Leading is doing something different.

1. Evaluate whether or not you've gained the rapport you want. If you have been successful;, the other person will follow your lead when *you* do something different from the mirroring gesture. That will be your signal that you've been successfully achieving rapport and that the other person is open to following your lead. You've been told this, however, only in a nonverbal way. You can now . . .

2. Send up a trial balloon (in selling, it's called a trial close) to see if the other person seems willing to accept your idea or proposal.

If you notice that the other person is not following your lead, then go back to pacing. This process of matching, pacing, and leading is a continuous one. You may mirror another person's posture for a while and notice if he or she follows your lead when you change position slightly. Then you can continue mirroring and leading.

SUMMARY

INFLUENCE = ATTENTIVENESS + FLEXIBILITY

People in general will be far more likely to respond to your influence when you work with good rapport. Therefore, you must be attentive to all their individual behaviors, from the way they breathe to the way they speak, learn and process information. You must watch and mirror these behaviors in a natural, subtle way. Your flexibility enables you to take the lead.

By establishing good rapport on a variety of levels and speaking the same language, best possible position to get others to respond favorably to your ideas and thus to achieve your goal.

Now you're a more tuned-in listener, a more aware and awake communication, a more strategic influencer. You're in charge now, with attentiveness, flexibility, and influence making a more powerful you.

Good luck and much success. If you keep practicing the few simple ideas on a daily basis, you will certainly enhance your chances to fulfill your every dream and goal.

NOTES

NOTES

NOTES

NOTES

OVER 150 BOOKS AND 35 VIDEOS AVAILABLE IN THE 50-MINUTE SERIES

50-Minute Series Books and Videos Subject Areas . . .

Management
Training
Human Resources
Customer Service and Sales Training
Communications
Small Business and Financial Planning
Creativity
Personal Development
Wellness
Adult Literacy and Learning
Career, Retirement and Life Planning

Other titles available from Crisp Publications in these categories

Crisp Computer Series
The Crisp Small Business & Entrepreneurship Series
Quick Read Series
Management
Personal Development
Retirement Planning